Enjoying Sport and Exercise

Sheila Hollins and Caroline Argent, illustrated by Catherine Brighton

Books Beyond Words
RCPsych Publications/St George's, University of London
LONDON

46 827 557 4

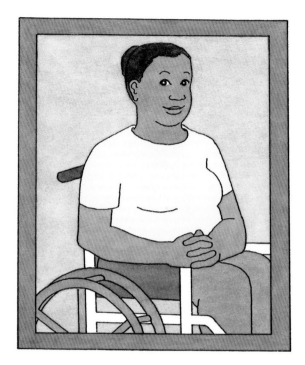

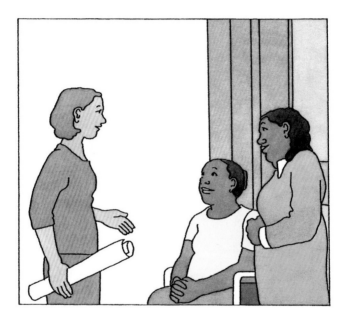

8

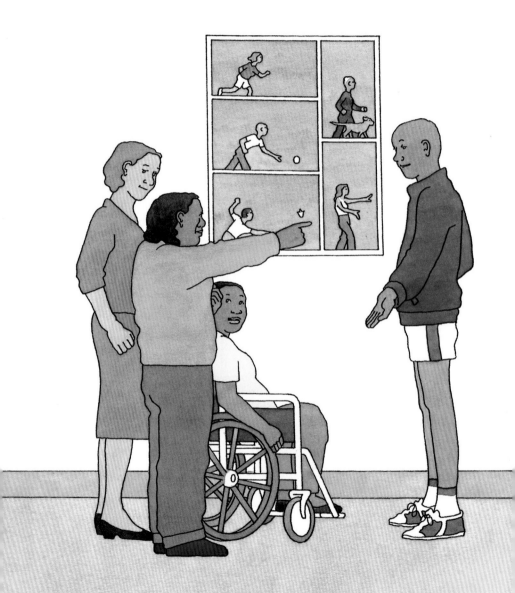

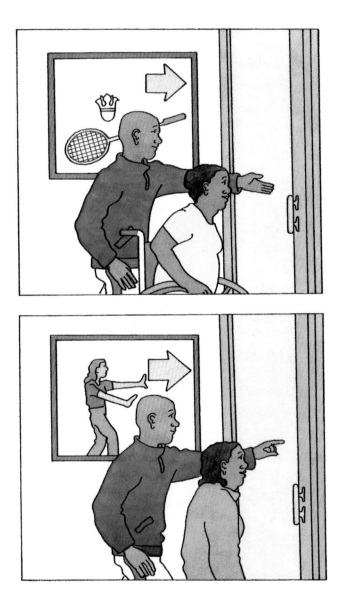

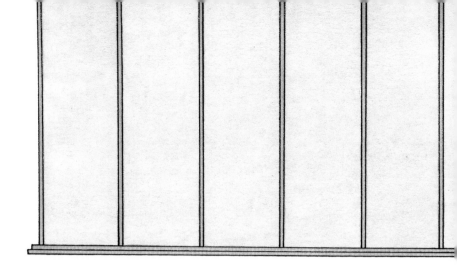

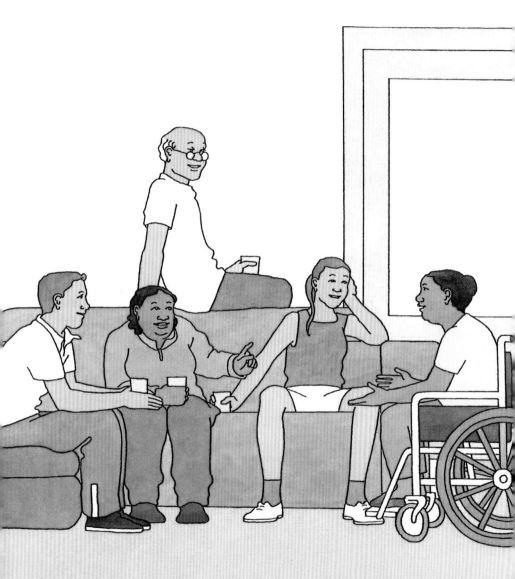

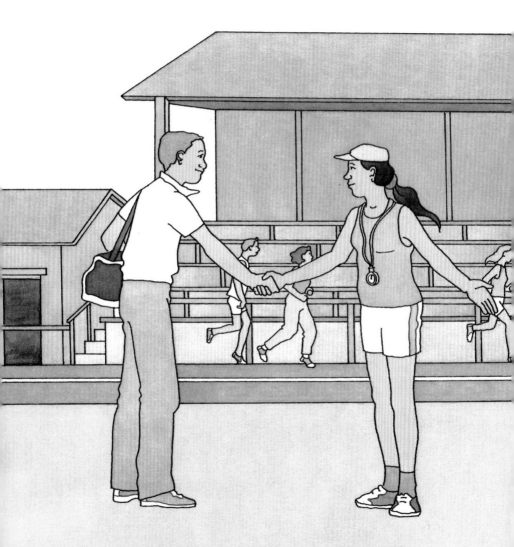

43

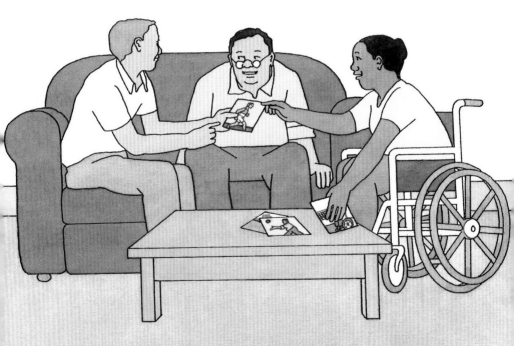

The following words are provided for readers or carers who want a ready-made story rather than tell their own

1. These people are bored, sitting there doing nothing. A woman comes in. She carries something. What is it?

2. The woman is called Emma. She shows them lots of things they can do. She says 'You can do sport and exercise. Look, you can go running, play a game with a racquet or walk a dog.'

3. This is Jasmine.

4. Jasmine thinks about doing sport. She thinks about badminton. Her parents are watching TV. They don't know she wants to try sport and exercise.

5. Jasmine tells them what she wants. 'I want to play badminton.' Mum thinks she can't do it because of her wheelchair.

6. Emma comes to Jasmine's home with a poster. She says 'This is how you do it. There is a coach at the sports centre who teaches people to play badminton.' Mum and Dad look pleased.

7. Emma goes to the sports centre. She explains to the coach that Jasmine uses a wheelchair to get around. He is surprised. 'Does she want to play badminton?' Emma says ' Yes. She can do it if you help her.'

8. They arrive at the sports centre – Emma, Jasmine and Jasmine's Mum. The coach asks 'What do you want to try?' Jasmine points to badminton and says she wants to do that.

9. Mum says she likes the look of tai chi, and the coach says 'You try that.'

10. The coach shows Jasmine to the badminton court. He shows Mum to the tai chi class. 'This is Tyler – he is your badminton partner.' Jasmine is ready to play. Look. She has taken the sides off her wheelchair.

11. The coach asks Jasmine which shuttlecock she wants to use. She chooses the big one. She practises with some shuttlecocks. The coach teaches her to aim at the red and white cone on the other side of the net.

12. There are four people playing together. Some are beginners. The shuttlecock is on the floor. Jasmine bends to pick it up.

13. They are all playing badminton. Jasmine hits the shuttlecock over the net.

14. Jasmine's Mum watches a tai chi class. She wants to join in.

15. Now she tries tai chi. She copies the teacher.

16. Their classes finish and they all relax together. They talk about badminton and tai chi.

17.   This is Charlie.

18.   Charlie sits in his kitchen. He is lonely. What can he do?

19.   Susan comes to see Charlie. She brings her dog with her. She is carrying a poster. Charlie invites her in.

20.   She shows him some pictures of sports. He wants to go bowling.

21.   They go out together. Charlie tries bowling. He throws the ball too high.

22.   Oh dear. That ball is going the wrong way.

23.   Charlie has had enough! It's too hard.

24.   He looks at some more pictures with Susan. She suggests dog walking.

25.   The dog is going too fast. Charlie holds him by the lead. He tries to keep up. It's fun.

26.   Charlie's friend is playing cricket in the park. They wave to each other. Charlie watches them play.

27.   The game is over. Charlie's friend invites them to have some tea.

28.   Charlie has a go. His friend bats him the ball. Charlie tries to catch the ball. It's hard but it gets easier if you practise. Charlie wants to come back and play again.

29. Susan and her dog walk home with Charlie. They enjoyed their day out.

30. This is James.

31. James is upset about something. He looks angry. Mary thinks he will break something soon.

32. James runs out of the house. He looks very cross.

33. The policeman says hello as James runs past.

34. James stops for a chat. He and the policeman walk back together.

35. James talks to the policeman. He tells him that he gets cross sometimes.

36. James says he loves running. The policeman can see he likes running.

37. The policeman says 'You can learn to run better. Go to a running track and get a coach.'

38. James goes out of his house. He carries a sports bag. He looks OK. He goes to a running club. He meets the coach.

39. The coach shows James what to do. She asks him to practise running on the track. He learns from her and he runs fast.

40. James goes home. He is tired and happy. He enjoys his bath.

41. It looks cold outside. It's autumn now. James runs in all kinds of weather. He wraps up warm and goes out. James runs with his coach.

42. It's time to go running again. James practises a lot. He runs in a race. He is a fast runner. Some of his friends watch him. The policeman sees him and waves.

43. Jasmine, Charlie and James talk about their new sports.

44. Photo time again!

45. They have a picnic in the park. Jasmine's Mum shows them some tai chi.

The benefits of sport and exercise

Anyone can help himself or herself keep fit and feel well by taking part in weekly exercise or sport. Taking part in sport and exercise can help you to cope with your worries, can help you to sleep, and can help you lose weight (if you also change the way you eat!). Taking part in exercise and sport can help you meet people outside your home and have fun. It can help a lot if you feel down, angry or sad. Some people have heart problems, some have breathing difficulties and many are overweight. Many people also smoke and eat a lot of fatty food with too much salt. Many people don't walk anywhere or do any exercise. Regular exercise can help with all of these problems.

Many people will have taken part in exercise at some time in their lives but do not do so at present. They may have moved, lost friends or groups of support. Previous activities may not have been taken up again and new activities not pursued or set up.

People also forget how much fun they had when doing sport and they forget other benefits like learning new skills, or having better concentration and self-confidence. Remember that it is going out of the house, meeting people and having fun in exercise and sport that makes people want to keep coming back, not just the exercise or keeping fit.

Starting something new is more successful if taken one step at a time. Planning carefully is more likely to lead to success and it will help people to build their confidence and knowledge.

What should supporters and carers do to help someone get started?

Use this book to help the person choose a sport or exercise. With their permission visit the sports centre or club yourself to meet the coach or organiser. Find out what is available for them. Accompany them the first few times they go to the activity until they feel confident and the coach is coaching them successfully. Support them to learn public transport routes to get there.

Step 1: What do you like?

When you know what you want, it is easier to find the right activity. Knowing what interests or excites someone can help them to find an exercise that matches their personality and that they will enjoy and maybe do again. For example, someone who does not like small or enclosed spaces but likes people and has a lot of energy might try outdoor sports such as athletics/running, cycling, football, tennis or softball. Someone who likes exciting things, who always wants to learn something new and gets bored easily, could try rambling or hill walking, dance, ice hockey, karate or judo, skiing, cycling, sailing or indoor climbing. If someone is quiet and does not like running around, they might enjoy bowls, kite flying, ten pin bowling, walking, archery, tai chi, qi gong, snooker, darts or table tennis.

Step 2: Before you start a new sport

Many people hesitate to start something new and so do not get round to doing any exercise or sport. Many have concerns about how fit they should be, what clothes to wear, who will go with them, how expensive it is, and will they be good enough? These are all normal feelings about doing something new, out of your normal routine. Once you have taken part a few times, it becomes easier and you will know what to wear, where to go and how to behave. Sometimes you may also stop because you get a cold or your work or college timetable gets in the way, but it is important to start again soon. Think about any worries you have and what support you need. Take it one step at a time.

Step 3: Where do you go and who do you ask?

When you ask about sports for people with learning disabilities at the town hall, in libraries or elsewhere, you may only be provided with a list of activities for disabled people and not a list of **all** the activities available. Often the variety and number of activities for people with disabilities is low. But you should ask for a full list of what sport and exercise classes are available in your area, so that you have more choice. You have the right to be included. There could be more than a hundred different types of exercise and sport sessions in your community! A lot of the information on what is available will not be provided in easy pictures and words. You may need someone to read the information to you and find the place on the map.

Step 4: Which activity?

When you have a list of what's on, how do you choose something to try? There will be different types of sports activities to meet different needs and abilities:

Do you need a disability sports club? Some sports have been developed with people with disabilities in mind like boccia, or are inclusive games, like new age kurling or power chair football.

Do you need a multisports club? This is a type of session where people get to play different sports each week and so it is a good introduction to sport and exercise. It helps people to learn basic sport skills, become fitter and gain confidence.

Or do you need a sports club which provides modified activity? This is when everyone is doing the same sport but with changes to the rules, area or equipment to include people of all abilities. This can be run either within a mainstream session or as a separate session for people with disabilities. This type of session is good to help people learn specific sports skills, to become more confident and take part in competitions if they want.

Or do you need a parallel activity in a mainstream sports club, where participants play the same game but different groups play the game in different ways and at different levels. This type of session is good for people who want to progress, play more often and compete.

Or maybe you need an open sports activity? These are activities that generally need little or no change to be made in order to ensure that everyone is included.

You may need to try a few different activities before you find the right one for you. If it doesn't work at first don't give up, keep trying until you find the right one.

Some different types of sports activities:

Karate, judo, jujitsu, golf, sailing, canoeing, rowing, cricket, running, volleyball, swimming, water polo, walking, parasailing, diving, skiing, snooker, cycling, table tennis, boccia, bowls, archery, basketball, canoeing, gymnastics, netball, ice-skating, fencing, tag rugby, new age curling, lawn bowls, ten pin bowling, football, tennis, trampolining, horse riding, badminton, fishing.

Disability sports:

Boccia, zone hockey, sledge hockey, wheelchair basketball, wheelchair rugby, wheelchair football, polybat, table cricket, motor activities training programme (MATP) – for people with profound or multiple learning disabilities.

Some different types of physical activities:

- dancing – disco dancing, line dancing, ballroom, aerobics
- walking – walking around the park, rambling in the countryside, walking home from shopping or visiting friends and relatives
- cycling – cycling to work, visiting friends, going to the shops
- fitness – weights, running/rowing machines, aerobics

- aqua (water) aerobics, chair-based exercise, tai chi, qi gong, rounders, tag rugby, skateboarding, kite flying, walking the dog, gardening, frisbee, rollerblading

Step 5: Preparation and getting ready

People who have not done exercise for a long time should go to the doctor first for a check up. If you have a health action plan you can also ask the doctor or nurse to advise or refer you to the sports centre and add it to your health plan.

For exercise to be of physical benefit, people need to take part in moderate intensity exercise. This is a level where you begin to sweat, can still talk while doing it, but don't feel out of breath. The overall aim is to be active three times a week, each time for about 30 minutes.

Gentle exercise like taking a walk is an excellent way to develop fitness. It makes your balance better and makes you more flexible. Yoga, tai chi, chair-based exercise, aqua (water) aerobics or a gentle beginners programme in a gym given to you by an instructor are all good for developing general fitness and mobility.

The food you eat is also an important part of getting fit. Remember to eat lots of fruit and vegetables – aim for five portions every day. Eat more fish, and cut down on saturated fat, sugar and salt – and drink plenty of fluid. Try to drink at least 6–8 cups (1.5–2 litres) daily and half of this should be water. Don't skip breakfast and please don't do exercise for at least an hour after eating a heavy meal!

Step 6: Making sessions accessible for you

Anyone new to sport or exercise needs coaching to learn the basic skills so they can take part.

Meet the instructor or coach before attending the first time to discuss what they can do to help you take part successfully. Often they will need some information about you to include you fully in a sports session. You can help them yourself by telling them what you can do and how they need to communicate with you to help you learn the rules and play the game.

Coaches can be reassured that once they get to know someone, it is likely that communication will become easier. They need to understand the new person and to make sure that they are meeting that person's needs fully.

Nearly all sport and exercise activities can be adapted and made accessible for a disabled person. Each has a skill sequence, rules and scoring, playing area and equipment that can easily be changed so that everyone can participate successfully.

Adapting the skill sequence means that the coach must look at the sports movements, break them down into smaller parts and find which ones someone cannot do. The coach can then look for different ways to change this step so that the person can learn a skill or the rules of a game and take part successfully. You may need to repeat a set of actions many times before the new skill becomes natural.

Adapting equipment might include using ramps to roll a ball, or a tee stand to hold a ball, so that you can hit the ball off it with your bat.

Adapting the rules might mean lowering the net or allowing a two-handed bounce in basketball.

Adapting an environment might mean making the playing court smaller or having people play in allocated zones.

Step 7: At the beginning of every exercise and sport session please remember to

- Begin slowly and build up, never push yourself too far or too fast.
- Warm up and cool down for 10 minutes before and after your activity.
- Never stop suddenly, always use a cooling down period to allow the heart rate to slow down, in its own time.
- Don't take part in exercise if you have just eaten a meal.
- Wear loose clothing that's right for what you are doing. Wear the right shoes – they should be flat with rubber soles and have no heels. The shoes should cover, protect and support your whole foot.

Step 8: Some possible setbacks

Typical setbacks you may have while doing sport or exercise include:

- Not enough inclusive sports and exercise opportunities because coaches don't know how to include a person with disabilities.
- Limited choice of sport activities for disabled people. People want a wide range of activities such as judo, cycling, basketball, dance, etc.

- Coaches and sports centre staff may not believe that people with learning disabilities can play sport and learn the rules.

- Sports information may not be available in easy pictures and words.

- Lack of transport training or buddy schemes.

- Lack of initiatives to support people to attend activities at different times of the day and at weekends.

- Not knowing about council-run sports centre membership card schemes which offer reduced rates or free access for people with disabilities.

- Most staff and carers are unaware of the social and emotional benefits of taking part in sport and exercise.

- Carers' and support workers' personal fears and discomfort about taking part in exercise and physical activity can be a real barrier to people who need support to access sports in the community.

- Getting involved in the community can take time to set up before it becomes routine. There are many things to upset the process such as staff changes, illness and frustration.

Where to find help and advice

English Federation of Disability Sport (EFDS)

The national body responsible for developing sport for all disabled people in England. It has ten regional offices. Website: http://www.efds.co.uk, telephone: 0161 247 5294.

London Sports Forum for Disabled People (LSF)

Develops sport and physical activity for disabled people in London. Website: http://www.londonsportsforum. org.uk, telephone: 020 7717 1699.

Special Olympics Great Britain

Local sports clubs and competition for people with learning disabilities all over the UK and Ireland. Website: http://www.sogb.org.uk/, telephone: 020 7247 8891, e-mail: info@sogb.org.uk.

Equality and Human Rights Commission

The Commission includes the work of the Centre for Racial Equality, Equal Opportunities Commission and the Disability Rights Commission. One of the key aims of the Commission is to end discrimination and harassment of people because of their disability. If you think you are being discriminated against, for example because adjustments have not been made to include you in an exercise or sport, then contact the Commission on their telephone helpline: 0845 604 6610 on Monday, Tuesday, Thursday and Friday 9 am to 5 pm; Wednesday 9 am to 8 pm; e-mail: info@equalityhumanrights.com.

Your local council sports development unit

Contact your local council and ask for the Sports and Recreation Department, which will have a list of non-disabled sports clubs and disability specific sessions you could try.

Inclusive Fitness Initiative (IFI)

A programme that supports the fitness industry to become more inclusive, catering for the needs of people with and without disabilities. Find your local Inclusive Fitness gym on their website: http://www.inclusivefitness.org.

Written materials

Taking Turns: Around Recreation and Leisure

by Alice Bradley (1999). Three booklets that help people find the right sport or exercise to match their personality. Includes templates to plan support. Available at £16.00 from BILD, Wolverhampton Road, Kidderminster, Worcestershire DY10 3PP, telephone: 015 6285 0251, and from Amazon at http://www.amazon.co.uk.

Community Recreation and People with Disabilities: Strategies for Inclusion

by S.J. Schleien, M.T. Ray & F.P. Green, published by Paul H. Brookes Publishing Co (1997, 2nd edition). This is an excellent, easy to use pre-exercise and inclusion planning tool. Available from Amazon at £35.99 (http://www.amazon.co.uk).

Your Good Health: Exercise

Published by BILD (1998). Appealing, colourful and easy to read text. Available from Amazon at £8.00 (http://www.amazon.co.uk).

What is a Learning Disability and Adapting your Coaching Style to Include People with Learning Disability

by Tracey Hickey (2006). Clear and simple pamphlets for sports coaches. Available free from Sutton Mencap, 8 Stanley Park Road, Wallington, London SM6 0EU.

Support Worker's Toolkit. Community sport and exercise

by Caroline Argent (2004). Information, advice and resources for support workers. Available at £10 from the London Sports Forum for Disabled People, Unit 2BO7, South Bank Technopark, 90 London Road, London SE1 6LN.

Social Inclusion Planner

by the National Development Team. Provides many tried and tested strategies to support social inclusion. Download free from http://www.ndt.org.uk/projectsN/SIPdl.htm

Learning Disability Qualification

A set of training modules appropriate to frontline staff who work with people with learning disabilities. Modules relevant to exercise and sport are: Unit 014 levels 2 & 3, Unit 022 levels 2 & 3, Unit 118 level 3, Unit 138 level 3. The price of each module varies. The qualification is in the process of changing, see the website for any new information (http://www.ldaf.org.uk).

Swimming Guidelines for Adults with Epilepsy

Booklet available free from Barnet Mencap, 35 Hendon Lane, London N3 1RT, telephone: 020 8349 3842.

Food... Fun, Healthy and Safe

by Sheila Hollins and Margaret Flynn, illustrated with full-colour pictures by Catherine Brighton (2003), in the Books Beyond Words series. It shows how choosing, cooking and eating food can be fun as well as healthy and safe. It includes general advice on eating well and outlines special diets. Available at £10 (includes postage and packaging) from the Royal College of Psychiatrists, 17 Belgrave Square, London SW1X 8PG, telephone: 020 7235 2351, website: http//www. rcpsych.ac.uk.

George Gets Smart

by Sheila Hollins, Margaret Flynn and Philippa Russell, illustrated by Catherine Brighton (2003). George's life changes when he goes running with his friends and workmates. He also learns the importance of keeping clean and smart. Books Beyond Words, available at £10 (as above) from the Royal College of Psychiatrists, 17 Belgrave Square, London SW1X 8PG, telephone: 020 7235 2351, website: http//www.rcpsych.ac.uk.

Acknowledgements

We thank our editorial advisors, Gary Butler, Trevor Duke, Stuart Dunn, Nigel Hollins and Keith Shortman, members of the Camden Parents Sports Group, the psychotherapy group at the Joan Bicknell Centre, Josie Lombardo and members of Safety Net People First and Active London Projects, for their ideas and advice about what was needed in the pictures.

We are grateful for the advice and support of our advisory group, which included representatives from Barnet Primary Care Trust, Camden Learning Disabilities Service, Westminster Primary Care Trust, Oxleas Foundation Trust, Hackney Independent Living Trust, Sutton Mencap and Ken Black from the Peter Harrison Centre for Disability Sport. The following gave their time most generously: Stephan Brusch, Mark Bradley, Frank Earley and Alison Pointu.

We are grateful to the London Sports Forum for Disabled People for having the idea for this project and who, with us, approached the Lloyds TSB Foundation for England and Wales without whose generous financial support this book would not have been possible.

Our special thanks go to Dorothea Duncan who is our managing editor and oversaw the whole project with exceptional patience.